SERMON OUTLINES on Great Doctrinal Themes

Charles R. Wood

Grand Rapids, MI 49501

Sermon Outlines on Great Doctrinal Themes

Published by Kregel Publications, a division of Kregel, Inc., P.O. Box 2607, Grand Rapids, MI 49501. Kregel Publications provides trusted, biblical publications for Christian growth and service. Your comments and suggestions are valued.

For more information about Kregel Publications, visit our web site at: www.kregel.com

Cover design: Frank Gutbrod

Library of Congress Cataloging-in-Publication
Sermon outlines on great doctrinal themes / by Charles R. Wood.

p. cm.

1. Sermons—Outlines, syllabi, etc. I. Title. II. Charles R. Wood.

BV4223.W663 1991 91-27157
252'.02—dc20

ISBN 0-8254-4123-4

2 3 4 5 / 04 03

Printed in the United States of America

Contents

List of Scripture Texts

Introduction

For a subject as absolutely essential as it clearly is, doctrine (more formally called *theology*) has long taken a beating in popularity among God's people. In more recent years, however, there has been a renewed interest in the systematic study of God's Word, especially among young people. J.I. Packer, James Montgomery Boice, R.C. Sproul, and others are certainly influential in this renewed doctrinal interest. Their popular style and serious scholarship have done much to rekindle interest in what has too long been a dormant subject. My own congregation, composed largely of younger people, has been enthusiastic about a recent series of sermons on various theological themes.

In this volume I have selected also Scriptures and sermons on Satan which reflect my conviction that Satan is far more influential in our world than we realize or admit.

Careful study of the Scripture passages included with each sermon will reap significant dividends both in facility of preaching and in depth of understanding. Several of these sermons can easily yield two or more messages when an entire sermon is developed from a single major point.

May the Lord, to whom the study of theology points, be pleased to greatly use these messages in both pulpit and pew.

CHARLES R. WOOD

A Word to Live By: Atonement

Romans 5:10–11

Introduction:

Yom Kippur is the Day of Atonement for Jews. Considering the fact that the word is used only once in the New Testament and not much more in the Old Testament, atonement is very important. It is actually a created word, created to describe a Biblical truth.

I. The Problem of Man

A. We have a BIG problem—the Bible makes it look very BAD with pictures it draws.
   1. He is a slave needing buy-back (Romans 7:14).
   2. He is an enemy needing placation (Colossians 1:21).
   3. He is a corpse needing resurrection (Ephesians 2:1, 5).
   4. He is a captive needing freedom (2 Timothy 2:26).
   5. He is a criminal needing pardon (Romans 7:22–25).

B. It is difficult to make our situation worse than it already is.

II. God's Provision

A. "Atonement" is translated only once in the New Testament.
   1. It is used in Romans 5:10–11.
   2. The word is used four other times.
   3. It is translated "reconcile."

B. Reconciliation is described in 1 Corinthians 7:11.
   1. It means to make peace between, bring back together.
   2. It assumes God and man are estranged but does something about it.

III. God's Procedure

A. The Old Testament word means "covering."
   1. It is seen in same word translated "mercy seat."
   2. Read Exodus 25:17–22.

B. The atonement is actually "covering."
   1. Read Leviticus 6.
   2. Blood of animal "covered" sin of the people.

C. The covering was only temporary until Christ.
   1. Animal blood *covered sin*.
   2. Christ's blood *washes sin away* (1 John 1:7).

Conclusion:

We are estranged from God. God has made provision for reconciliation. Reconciliation is through the blood of Christ, and the only way to be "covered" is to accept Him.

Just As if I . . .

Romans 5:1–11

Introduction:

Sometimes we teach children short sayings. For instance—justified means "Just as if I'd never sinned." It is not very theological, but it is not too bad as a definition.

I. Definition

A. The setting is the courtroom.
   1. The prosecutor reads charges.
   2. The person admits guilt.
   3. A sentence is required ("soul that sinneth . . .").
   4. The judge declares not guilty.

B. We are more than not guilty.
   1. All failure/sin is forgiven.
   2. We are viewed as if having kept the law.
   3. We are granted additional privileges.

II. Method

A. Our sin/failure is not just glossed over.

B. Christ took care of both.
   1. He paid penalty for sins.
   2. He fulfilled law for righteousness (Romans 10:4).
   3. He both lived and died for us—both aspects are fully cared for.

III. Application

A. How does what He did get credited to our account?
   1. It is credited to us when we accept Him.
   2. When we accept Christ, we accept what He did as well.
   3. We are justified by grace through faith.

B. God does it by grace, and it is applied by faith.

IV. Benefits

A. Justification gives standing with God.

B. Justification opens box of blessings (Romans 5:1-11).

C. Judgment is thus moved up and completed (case can't be reopened).

D. Justification grants status that can't be lost.

Conclusion:

Justification is a major Bible theme. There is only one way to get justified. You might earn it by keeping the law, but no one can keep the law. You can only draw on what Christ has done, and that is done through faith. Are you justified?

Our Light Affliction

2 Corinthians 4:17

Introduction:

Are you kidding, Paul? What do you mean, "our light affliction?" Some of us are going through heavy affliction; where do you come off calling it light? Paul is writing under inspiration and knows whereof he speaks. Whatever your affliction, it is really light. Here are seven reasons why that is true:

I. **Your affliction is light when compared with that of many others.**
   A. No matter how heavy, there are others with worse.
   B. Paul endured incredible afflictions—he speaks from experience.

II. **Your affliction is light compared with your deserts.**
   A. It is unworthy to be compared to the woes of the lost (slightly revealed in story of rich man and Lazarus).
   B. You actually deserve the woes of hell (and would have them were it not for the grace of God in Christ).

III. **Your affliction is light compared to that of your Lord.**
   A. He drained an ultimate cup of woe.
   B. Thus the One who regulates our afflictions knows exactly what afflictions really are.

IV. **Your affliction is light compared with the blessings you enjoy.**
   A. We possess:
      1. Salvation.
      2. Righteousness.
      3. Adoption.
      4. The privileges of the children of God.
      5. The assurance of future glories.
   B. No amount of affliction can take these blessings away (or outweigh them either).

V. **Your affliction is light in comparison to its benefits to you.**
   A. It proves the power of sustaining grace.
   B. It is designed of God to make changes in you.
      1. It can drive out sin.
      2. It can develop character.
      3. It can deepen your walk with God.

VI. Your affliction is light because of its relative brevity.

A. "Which is but for a moment"—it is not lasting.

B. It must be viewed as relative.

1. Compare it to the overall span of life.
2. Compare it to the reach of eternity.

VII. Your affliction is light in comparison to the glory to be revealed.

A. Paul refers to "a far more exceeding and eternal weight of glory."

B. Handling the affliction right can increase the weight of glory.

1. It can make us more what God wants us to be.
2. It can increase the weight of the reward awaiting us.

Conclusion:

Our afflictions are much a matter of focus. Focus on the afflictions, and they become heavy. Focus on what God is doing through them, and they lose weight. Whatever it is that you are going through, will you see it through God's eyes? Or will you see it as some heavy weight? Paul says, "For our light affliction which is but for a moment," and we had better agree with him.

Why Baptists Are Baptists

Acts 8:26–40

Introduction:

Baptism must be significant to at least one group of Christians because they call themselves Baptists. What do Baptists believe about baptism?

I. The Only Example of Biblical Baptism

A. It excludes Christ's which was different from ours in several ways.

B. Trace the story of the Ethiopian official.

1. Notice the stress (vv. 36–37).
2. Notice the sequence:
   a. Salvation then baptism.
   b. Consistent where baptism is mentioned.
3. Notice the statements:
   a. "See here is [a] water" (v. 36).
   b. "And they went down both into the water" (v. 38).
   c. "And he baptized him" (obviously in the water) (v. 38).
   d. "And when they were come up out of the water" (v. 39).
4. Notice the symbolism:
   a. A picture of death, burial, resurrection of Christ.
   b. A picture of washing away of sins.

II. The Language of Biblical Baptism

A. Notice the meaning of the word.

1. Baptism is not an English word.
2. It means to immerse.
3. It can mean so in entire New Testament.

B. Notice the clear teaching of Scripture (Rom. 6:3–5).

1. Its symbolism is very obvious.
2. It is totally lost on any other form of baptism.

C. It is derived versus direct teaching.

1. There is a case for other positions.
2. All other kinds of baptism are based on derived arguments.
3. Immersion is based on direct teaching.
4. Always prefer direct teaching when it is available.

III. The Clarity of the Baptism Commandment (Matt. 28:18–20)

A. Notice the sequence:
   1. "Teach"—make disciples of.
   2. "Baptize."
   3. "Teach"—instruct.

B. Notice the clear intention:
   1. If we are commanded to baptize those of whom we make disciples, then those who are discipled are obviously intended to be baptized.
   2. "Teaching to observe all things which I have commanded" also includes the commandment to baptize.

C. Notice the importance of obedience:
   1. It has nothing to do with actual salvation.
   2. It is a clear commandment.
   3. As a commandment, you should either obey or have a clear reason for not doing so (other than upbringing, etc.).

Conclusion:

Have you ever been biblically baptized? Have you ever been converted?

The Lordship of Christ

John 20:24–29

Introduction:

Are we saved simply by trusting the saving work of Christ, or must we recognize the Lordship of Christ to be saved? The debate has arisen because there is so much "shotgun" evangelism, and so few who profess salvation appear to have any understanding. We still must take a stand. We are saved by the saving work of Christ alone, but we should be moving converts quickly to an understanding of the Lordship of Christ. Thomas didn't start out very well, but he quickly came to understand what it was all about.

I. Thomas's doubt was inexcusable.

- A. He was absent when he should have been present.
- B. He should have known—Christ had said enough.
- C. He had rejected the witness of ten brethren that he should have trusted.

II. Christ's patience was unbelievable.

- A. He is totally tender with Thomas.
- B. He rebukes his unbelief:
  1. He does so tenderly.
  2. He does so because he needed it.
- C. He condescends to Thomas's request and invites his touch.

III. Tremendous themes are unmistakable.

- A. He claims deity—Jesus Christ is God.
  1. He repeatedly claimed so in Scripture.
  2. Any other position is untenable.
- B. He claims dominion—"Lord" in the sense of sovereignty.
  1. He has the right to rule.
  2. The "Lord" *owns* His right to rule.
- C. He calls for discipleship—"Lord" in the sense of teacher, master.
  1. A "disciple" is one who follows, learns from, or patterns after.
  2. A disciple must own Him as final authority.
- D. He calls for devotion—sense of love.
  1. It is not just because He is Lord.
  2. It is because of what His Lordship provided.

E. He calls for deference—deals with response to Lordship.
   1. I must submit to Him.
   2. I must submit to His authority.

IV. Powerful lessons are unavoidable.

A. It provides solid evidence of resurrection reality.
   1. This is the testimony of a doubter.
   2. Few things in history are as well authenticated.

B. It is a clear indication about His concern.
   1. It extends to individuals.
   2. It provides a caution to us.

C. There is an obvious lesson on the treatment of people.
   1. Note His incredible patience with Thomas.
   2. It challenges our tendency to give up on people.

D. It conditions our response to Him.
   1. We should respond the same.
   2. The order of response should be:
      a. First to His saving work.
      b. Then to His Lordship.

Conclusion:

It is great that Thomas came to belief, but you can be greater than Thomas. Notice the message of verse 29. Is He your Savior? Is He your Lord?

You Are the Church

1 Corinthians 3:9–13

Introduction:

A lovely building is not a church. All the beams, joists, decking, pews, seats, pulpit furniture, carpet, fixtures, woodwork, organ, piano, speaker system, chalkboards, easels, and podiums do not make a church. These merely form a church building or the building where the church meets.

I. You are the church.
- A. No building is ever mentioned in the NT.
- B. The building is not essential.
- C. What is the truth—you are God's building.
  1. The church is people.
  2. You are the key issue in the church.

II. Your foundation has already been laid.
- A. Paul says, "I have laid the foundation."
- B. There is only one foundation that can be laid.
  1. Everyone who has a foundation has the same one.
  2. If you don't have the one foundation, you don't have any foundation at all.
- C. Christ is the one foundation—faith in Him gives you this foundation.

III. You are responsible for building the superstructure.
- A. You build on that one foundation.
  1. The foundation is the same.
  2. The superstructures are different.
- B. You have the choice of various materials.
  1. Materials are detailed here.
  2. Materials are readily available.
- C. You are building with such things as:
  1. Conduct
  2. Character
  3. Communication
  4. Commitment
  5. Contribution

IV. Your workmanship will be tried.
- A. It will happen "at that day"—the "Day of the Lord."
- B. Your building will be manifest.
  1. It will be subjected to the fire of judgment.
  2. What you have truly built will be revealed.

a. There will be a discerning.
b. The true character of building will be revealed.

C. "Let every man take heed how he builds."
1. Our building is incredibly important.
2. The architect might do differently if he knew trial coming.

Conclusion:

You are the real church building. Your foundation has been laid in Christ. How you build is incredibly important.

O Thou of Little Faith

Matthew 14:31

Introduction:

"O thou of little faith"—repeated four times in Matthew 6:30; 8:26; 14:31; 16:8, and all four times it was said to disciples. "Great faith" is commended twice (Matt. 8:10; 15:28). There is a gulf between no faith and little faith, but there is only a distance between little faith and great faith.

I. **Christ gently censures little faith.**
   A. It is often found where we might expect greater things.
      1. We see it in Peter and the disciples as a whole.
      2. These men had seen and known too much to be like this.
   B. It is dependent on appearances.
      1. Peter's faith did not become little; it was little, and the situation merely revealed it.
      2. Little faith wants a "token for good"; strong faith believes God's bare Word without sign or token.
   C. It is affected by surrounding circumstances.
      1. Peter tended to live by feeling and sight; Peter was okay until he focused on the storm. Weak faith limits us by our environment.
      2. Strong faith knows where its true standing is and focuses there—on God and His Word.
   D. It tends to exaggerate its peril.
      1. Peter never thought of swimming; it was walk or sink for him.
      2. Little faith tends to build "worst case" scenarios.
   E. It tends to be unreasonable.
      1. Faith is reasonable; unbelief is unreasonable.
      2. If it is worth trusting at all, it is worth trusting to the full.
   F. It often gets a wetting.
      1. Weak faith is a great fabricator of terrors.
      2. Peter got wet, but it was his own little faith which was responsible for it.

II. **Christ tenderly commends little faith.**
   A. It is faith—the weakest faith is still faith.
      1. Jesus Himself acknowledges that it is faith.
      2. He rebuked Peter because of little faith but smiled on him because of faith.

B. It attempts to get to Jesus.
   1. Peter did not step out just to walk, but to walk to Jesus.
   2. "He who seeks Jesus has his face turned in the right direction."
C. It usually turns to prayer in time of trouble.
   1. It knows where its help lies.
   2. Peter didn't try swimming; he turned to prayer.
D. It is always safe because it brings us near Jesus.
   1. Peter was not saved by strength of faith but by the hand of his master.
   2. It senses turning toward Him and responds.
E. It tends to recover and renew itself.
   1. For all his little faith, Peter walked on water.
   2. Take heart in the darkest of nights—the sun will shine again.

III. Christ earnestly commends great faith.

A. It is sometimes found where we least expect it.
   1. It is found among those outside Israel.
   2. It is sometimes found in unexpected places.
B. It perseveres in seeking the Lord.
   1. The woman would not take "no" for an answer.
   2. Great faith doesn't stop until it has an answer.
C. It sees light in the deepest darkness.
   1. It is not dependent on indications.
   2. It believes in God for God's sake.
D. It enters into prevailing prayer.
   1. Great faith does not let go until it has found assurance.
   2. Great faith has the keys of heaven on its chain.
E. It delights our Lord.
   1. He smiled at the woman but probably not at Peter.
   2. He said, "Be it unto thee as thou wilt."
F. It confers great benefits on others.
   1. Woman secured salvation for her child.
   2. We could accomplish much more for others with great faith.

Conclusion:

What kind of faith do you have? What kind of faith do you want to have? How will you move on to achieve it?

Faith

Hebrews 11:1–3

Introduction:

People believe strange things like reincarnation, astrology, occultism, pyramid power, and healers and call it all "faith." How different from what the Bible says about faith.

I. Faith is believing.

A. "The substance of things hoped for."
   1. "Substance"—surety—being sure.
   2. "Being sure of what we hope for."

B. "The evidence of things not seen."
   1. "Evidence"—certainty—being certain.
   2. "Being certain of what we do not see."

C. It is much more objective than usually held.
   1. It is based on idea of unseen world.
   2. It is based on knowledge/fact not feelings; "feelings are the enemy of faith."

II. Faith is believing in God.

A. It must be in someone or thing to have meaning.
   1. Much faith today is in faith itself.
   2. Faith without basis is irrational.

B. We see biblical faith in Hebrews 11:6.
   1. We must believe that God exists.
   2. We must believe that He can and will do something ("Faith is not believing that God can, but that He will").

C. Christian faith requires facts for meaning.
   1. The Bible is not only source of revelation.
   2. The Bible is only place that interprets it.
   3. The Bible is absolutely necessary for meaningful Christian faith.
   4. Christian faith is the only meaningful religious faith there is.

III. Faith is believing in God enough to do certain things.

A. Act on His promises.
   1. Be sure they are properly understood.
   2. Be sure all else is in order.
   3. "If there are ways and means, there is not faith."

B. Obey His commandments.
   1. It often involves difficulty.

a. It runs counter to our thinking.
b. It goes against our desires.
c. It creates discomfort.

2. Faith can act because it believes that God knows best what is best.
3. Faith is the issue in much disobedience.

C. Accept His Word.

1. God is very plain:
   a. "Without faith . . ." (Hebrews 11:6).
   b. ". . . not of works . . ." (Ephesians 2:9).
   c. "Except a man . . ." (John 3:3).
2. There is no salvation without faith; no faith without accepting His Word.
3. Salvation must be God's way or not at all.

Conclusion:

Christianity is not "pie in the sky by and by." Christianity is belief in the existence, ability, and willingness of God to the point that I live by His promises, obey His commands, and accept His Word as final on any matter.

Words and Phrases

Ephesians 4:32

Introduction:

We stress forgiveness in a theological sense. We give little thought to it on a personal level. Forgiveness is tremendously important in interpersonal concerns.

I. The Meaning of "Forgiveness"

A Note the pattern—Ephesians 4:32.
1. Our forgiveness must be like His.
2. He goes on record regarding it (Isa. 43:24; Jer. 31:34).

B. Note the promise.
1. He promises not to remember our sins against us anymore (He will no longer hold them against us).
2. He does not say He will forget them.

C. Note the premise—there is a difference between forgetting and not remembering.
1. Forgetting is passive and can't be controlled by the will.
2. Not remembering is active and can be controlled (not bringing up a matter again no matter what).

D. Note the principle.
1. Forgiveness is a promise not to bring a matter up again:
   a. To the person involved.
   b. To others.
   c. To one's self.
2. It means not talking about it and not brooding about it.

II. The Nature of "Apology"

A. Note its status.
1. Apology is the usual method of dealing with interpersonal problems.
2. It is not Biblical concept.
3. It has different meaning in Scripture.
4. Apology is the world's substitute for forgiveness.

B. Note its shortcomings.
1. It tends to be defensive.
2. It tends to be a vehicle for avoidance.
   a. It only tells your feelings.
   b. It does not request any action.
   c. It makes no commitment.

d. It makes no provision for putting matter to rest.
e. It does not resolve the matter in any way.

C. Note its substitution.
1. What is required for forgiveness?
2. An apology completely evades the issue.

III. The Accuracy of "Forgive and Forget"

A. Note its essence.
1. We are to forgive and "willfully not remember."
2. "Forgetting" makes forgiveness unnecessarily complicated.

B. Note its error.
1. It is not Biblical at all.
2. To try to forget is to fail.
3. Forgiveness not based on our ability to forget.

C. Note its encouragement.
1. Forgiveness is the only way to "willfully not remember."
2. Forgive and you will learn to not remember.

Conclusion:

Forgiveness is a promise not to bring something up again or to use it against a person. An apology is a poor substitute for forgiveness as it doesn't deal with issues and it doesn't do what Bible says necessary in order to be forgiven. "Forgive and forget" is true only to the degree that forgetting is the result of forgiving and using our will to "not remember."

There's No Comparison

Isaiah 40:18, 25; 46:5

Introduction:

We constantly deal in comparisons, but comparisons break down regarding God. To whom will you liken God? What likeness will you compare to Him? To whom shall God be equal? To whom can we compare God to make a likeness? The prophet brings us face to face with realities.

I. **We can't compare God to anything/anyone** (v. 12).
   A. Likenesses are possible for illustration.
   B. Comparisons are impossible.
      1. To the ocean? (He can hold all moisture in His hand).
      2. To the heavens? (He measures heavens by ruler in His hand).
      3. To the earth? (He puts the dust in a measure).
      4. To the mountains? (He holds scales that weigh mountains).

II. **We can't understand God** (vv. 13–14).
   A. We can only KNOW Him as He reveals Himself:
      1. In conscience.
      2. In the natural world.
      3. In the Word of God.
   B. It says nothing about understanding Him (55:8–9).

III. **We can't fathom God.**
   A. Explain concept of "fathom": six foot length of rope used to measure depth—get to bottom of.
   B. Amply illustrated:
      1. By study of the Word.
      2. By computer technology—novice knows more of computers than man knows of God.

IV. **We can't outsmart God.**
   A. Explain the basic idea of being smarter than someone.
   B. We are never smarter than God.
      1. His knowledge is unlimited to point of completeness.
      2. Our knowledge is always limited.

V. **We can't escape God.**
   A. We are ultimately confronted by Him.
      1. Time lapse proves nothing.
      2. Confrontation is certain.

B. We will finally be held accountable.
   1. There will be an accounting.
   2. We are filling the pages now even though we may deny future accountability.

VI. We can't resist God.

A. Men and women constantly try to resist God.

B. Resistance is another indication of His incomparability.
   1. We resist by His allowance.
   2. He will call us to account for it.

Conclusion:

The Prophet asks: To whom will you liken God? What likeness will you compare to Him? To whom shall God be equal? To whom can we compare God to make a likeness? The answer is *nothing* and *no one*. In what areas are you being unrealistic?

The Secret Curse

Psalm 32:3–4

Introduction:

These verses describe intense suffering and remind us that some of the most intense suffering is in the mind. This suffering is the result of guilt as someone has called guilt "the secret curse." Many suffer from guilt, and we want to look at the subject in a helpful manner.

I. The Curse of Guilt

A. It has physical effects.
   1. "Bones"—body.
   2. "Waxed old"—wear out, decay (cf. Ps. 51:8).

B. It causes inner turmoil.
   1. "Roaring"—noise of suffering.
   2. Used of lion—often roars when in trouble.

C. It creates continuous conflict.
   1. "All the day long."
   2. The entire day or period of time.

D. It causes inescapable suffering.
   1. "Day and night."
   2. Has reference to light/darkness: no escape.

E. It creates a sense of divine disfavor.
   1. "Thy hand was heavy upon me."
   2. "Heavy" has meaning of burdensome (cf. Ps. 51:11–12).

F. It creates an inner barrenness.
   1. "My moisture turned into drought of summer."
   2. "If we won't face sin, God may dry it out of us."

II. The Cause of Guilt

A. Guilt was the result of what David had done:
   1. Lust
   2. Adultery/Immorality
   3. Deception
   4. Murder
   5. Cover-up

B. Guilt was the result of what David feared:
   1. Self-exposure—actually facing what he had done
   2. Public exposure
   3. God's punishment

C. Does all guilt arise out of wrong conduct?
    1. Some may arise out of failure to live up to expectations.
    2. Far more arises out of what we know is wrong.

III. The Cure for Guilt

A. Confession is step one.
    1. "When I kept silence"—failure to confess.
    2. Psalms 51:1-5 shows full extent of confession (note how he felt about what he had done).
    3. Why we don't confess:
        a. Personal pride.
        b. Hope conviction will die of itself.
        c. Hope that troubles will end of themselves.
        d. Hope that passage of time will bring relief.
        e. Hope that busyness/activity will soothe spiritual anguish.
        f. Tendency to self-vindication and rationalization.

B. Repentance is step two.
    1. It is some clear evidence that something has changed.
    2. It is very evident in Psalm 51:17.
    3. It is often the missing element in modern times.

C. Forgiveness is God's response to us.
    1. Note the obvious freedom found by David in rest of Psalm (esp. vs. 11).
    2. Forgiveness is a gift conferred by God in Christ.
    3. Then why don't I feel forgiven?—
        a. Because of my wounded pride.
        b. Because the matter is still an unsettled issue.

Conclusion:

Guilt is truly the secret curse; it does terrible things to us. It is incredibly common, caused by failing to face issues in our lives. It is cured only by confession, repentance, and forgiveness. Have you really dealt with what has caused your guilt, or are you trying to deal with the feelings of guilt without facing the issue?

The Stamp of the Spirit

Romans 8:14–17

Introduction:

And the war goes on . . . between the flesh and the Spirit. We are told what the Spirit and flesh are like. Thus we see the one we should follow. We are also told what the Spirit does for us (vv. 14–17).

I. **The Spirit leads** (v. 14).
   A. The Spirit gives us direction.
      1. Note Paul's experience in Acts 16.
      2. The direction is rarely alone and never contradictory.
      3. The Spirit persuades rather than forces.
      4. The Spirit becomes a controlling influence.
   B. The Spirit leads us into truth (Jn. 16:13).
      1. It has to do with Word of God.
      2. The Holy Spirit assists us in understanding the Word.
      3. Note further teaching in 1 Corinthians 2:12.
   C. The Spirit leads us into holiness.
      1. It is shown here and in Galatians 5:18.
      2. Note the entire sweep of context.

II. **The Spirit adopts** (v. 15).
   A. Note the characteristics of adoption.
      1. It bestows objective standing.
      2. It is permanently valid.
      3. It rests on loving purposes and grace of God.
   B. It establishes family relationship as well:
      1. Sons—statement of legal standing.
      2. Children—term of family relationship.
      3. "Abba"—closeness of relationship.
   C. It involves an inheritance.
      1. Even adopted slave shared inheritance.
      2. It follows a course:
         a. Slave to sin.
         b. Child of God.
         c. Heir to His riches.
      3. If we share cost of discipleship, we shall share glory.

III. The Spirit bears witness (vv. 16–17).

A. It is a coincidental witness.
   1. The Spirit's witness strikes a cord with the testimony of our human spirit.
   2. Both witnesses agree.

B. It is a confirmed witness.
   1. There is an internal witness.
   2. The internal is not too trustworthy.
   3. The witness of Word confirms.

C. It is a comforting witness.
   1. It assures us that we are the children of God.
   2. It assures us that we are joint-heirs.
   3. It assures us of future glorification.

Conclusion:

Paul says, "go the way of the Spirit," not only because of the great contrast, but because He leads us, He adopts us, and He testifies within us. Why do you continue to run after the flesh?

Unchanging and Unchangeable

Malachi 3:6

Introduction:

We live in times of great change, and more is on the way. It makes the future frightening, but here is a message of hope.

I. God is unchanging in His essence.
- A. Everything changes.
- B. God does not change.
  1. His essential essence stays same.
  2. Even the events of Christmas did not change Him.

II. God is unchanging in His attributes.
- A. All His characteristics stay the same.
- B. No difference in Old Testament/New Testament God.
- C. What He has done, He can do.

III. God is unchanging in His plans.
- A. He has a plan.
  1. We can see an analogy from human activity.
  2. This is the clear teaching of Scripture.
- B. His plan is unchanging.
  1. There are no surprises for God.
  2. Sometimes He puts in options for man, but they are part of His plan.

IV. God is unchanging in His promises.
- A. God's promises never change.
  1. They sometimes appear to.
  2. The change is in us.
- B. There is caution on promises.
  1. Be sure the promise is for you.
  2. Throw yourself on the promises that are yours.

V. God is unchanging in His threatenings.
- A. This is the reverse side of promises.
  1. Note His dark promises.
  2. There are many of these in Scripture.
- B. Here is an example:
  1. "He that believeth not is damned."
  2. Notice what it does and does not say.

VI. God is unchanging in the objects of His love.

A. He loves those who are His children.
B. We become children through belief.

Conclusion:

God is unchanging! What a tremendous encouragement in the midst of our changing world.

The Mercy of God

Nehemiah 9

Introduction:

There often appears to be a difference between God in the Old and New Testament. If God is the same, how can this be? It is usually explained that God deals with people differently in different times, but God is much more merciful in the Old Testament than it appears. A study of God's mercy as recited by Nehemiah can show us some important truths for our lives.

I. The children of Israel hold up a mirror for us.

A. They were specially favored but specifically ungrateful.
   1. They transgressed against light and love, instruction and illumination, wooing and warning, entreaty and rebuke.
   2. With the Lord before their eyes, they refused to see Him; with wonders in front of them, they refused to believe Him.
   3. Given so much of God, we continue to sin with every sin specifically against light.

B. They were dependent on God for everything but intensely proud of their own abilities.
   1. "If any people in the world ought to have been humble . . ."
   2. They were on God's welfare yet proudly claimed things for themselves.
   3. All we have is of God, yet we take credit for it and hold it as if it were something we produced.

C. They enjoyed a kind fatherhood but were deliberately rebellious.
   1. It was not mistakes or errors but deliberate disobedience (vv. 16–17).
   2. They would listen to everyone but their God.
   3. Most of our sin is not mistake or inadvertent error; it is deliberate rebellion against God.

D. They were singularly blessed yet crassly unmindful of what the Lord had done for them.
   1. They were constantly plagued by the crime of unbelief.
   2. God had delivered greatly; the slightest trouble or difficulty, their faith disappeared—what God had done had no effect.

3. Each new trial causes us to forget God's significant past blessings and to throw down our faith.

E. They had great spiritual privilege but committed an act of apostasy.
   1. They organized to go back to Egypt (appointed a leader).
   2. They forgot the degradation and servitude.
   3. We are guilty of the same thing every time we turn back to things we have renounced at the direction of the Holy Spirit.

F. They had specific commands yet fell into idolatry.
   1. They set up a molten calf (v. 18).
   2. They attributed to the calf things which the Lord had done.
   3. We may be more guilty of replicating this than any of the sins of Israel—we are constantly setting up idols in our lives.

II. The response of God shows His mercy.

A. He shows mercy to His children (who says The Old Testament God was different?).
   1. He continued to guide them while in their sins (v. 19), and we continue to know His guidance even when sinful.
   2. He continued to teach them while they arrogantly resisted (v. 20), and we have the ministry of the Holy Spirit even when wrong.
   3. He continued to provide for them while they were asserting their own rebellious independence (v. 20), and without His provision we would have nothing.
   4. He sustained them until the end and brought them to the promised land (vv. 21, 24–25), and He will do the same for us regardless.

B. He even shows His mercy to the unconverted.
   1. He extends love to people yet in their sins.
   2. He makes no conditions on His love.
   3. He actually provides Himself the things He demands of man (sinlessness, righteousness, etc.).

III. His mercy calls forth a response from us.

A. Note the instructive conduct of the children of Israel.
   1. In the wilderness they simply responded by piling provocation upon provocation (mercy was answered with more offenses).

    2. In the return they framed a covenant of commitment (10:28-39 with v. 29 summarizing the heart of it).
B. Note the response it calls forth from us.
    1. Some theologians fear teaching the mercy of God; they are afraid we will act as the Israelites did.
    2. Remember that there was another band of Israelites which acted properly, and we should follow their lead (show gratitude, display humility, exemplify submission, develop memory, cleave to the new ways of the Spirit, tear down our idols).

Conclusion:

God's mercy is part of His character. He can't do otherwise. Our response ought to be like that of the people in Nehemiah's day. We should covenant to walk in the ways of the Lord and to refuse every attempt to wean us away from it.

Repentance

Luke 15:11–24

Introduction:

Two questions: Is repentance necessary to salvation? Can a person be restored to leadership after a failure? They seem unrelated, but they are related through the subject of repentance.

I. The Meaning of Repentance

A. It is usually thought to be sorrow for sin.

B. The biblical meaning is different.

1. It is simply change of mind especially as regards sin/God.
2. It involves a recognition/regret for past sin and a desire/effort for change.
3. It is shown in life by fruit.

II. The Demonstration of Repentance

A. He realized his desperate condition—"He came to himself."

B. He made a mental determination to change his course—"I will arise and go to my father."

C. He made a decisive act—breaking away and going back—"He arose and came to his father."

D. He came with absolute humility—"I am no more worthy to be called a son."

E. He openly, unreservedly, unqualifiedly confessed his sin—"I have sinned to the very heaven, and my sin is against the best of fathers."

III. The Issue in Repentance

A. Is repentance required for salvation?

1. The question should be: "Is repentance part of salvation?"
2. It is hard to conceive of salvation without some recognition of sin.

B. Can a leader who has fallen be restored to a position of leadership?

1. Proper question: "Has the leader shown any genuine evidence of repentance?"
2. Restoration without repentance will issue in repeated offenses.
3. We can't discuss restoration until the issue of repentance settled.

Conclusion:

Without repentance—like the prodigal—there can be no restoration or reconciliation. Do you need to repent? Have you repented?

Doers, Not Hearers Only

James 1:22–27

Introduction:

The most exciting place in town should not be a football stadium. It should be any church that preaches the Word of God. This excitement is obviously of a different nature. Unfortunately, this is seldom true in any way.

I. The Essence of the Christian Life

- A. The things that it is not:
  1. It is not Christian experience.
  2. It is not prayer—important as that is.
  3. It is not witnessing.
- B. The thing that it is—the Bible:
  1. It is obedience to the Word of God.
     - a. It involves knowing what the Bible says.
     - b. It involves doing/not doing what the Bible says we should.
  2. It is the practice of the Word of God.
     - a. It is putting Bible principles into practice in life.
     - b. It is developing what we don't have that the Bible says we should have.

II. The Excitement of the Christian Life

- A. The experience of God's blessing is exciting!
  1. It emphasizes the importance of answered prayer.
  2. It emphasizes importance of spiritual victories:
     - a. Temptations withstood.
     - b. Sins conquered.
     - c. Souls won, etc.
- B. The expectations of the Word are exciting!
  1. There are things we must do and things we must not do.
  2. The "must do" becomes the "can do."
     - a. If God commands it, we can do it.
     - b. This makes a commandment very exciting.
     - c. When we say "I can't," we make God a liar.

III. The Exercise of the Christian Life

- A. Living by Biblical principles is exercise.
  1. All decisions should be made on basis of Biblical teaching.
  2. It implies sufficient knowledge to have basis.

B. Putting the Bible into practice is exercise.

C. How to do it:

  1. Select something to be worked on.
  2. Choose some specific way of doing it.
  3. Do that thing (21 days if you want it a habit).
  4. Make that practice part of your life.

Conclusion:

Christianity tends to become a drag for many people, but it ought to be continuously exciting and challenging. Your response to the Word of God will do much to determine the level of your spiritual energy! Is your spiritual life bland or blossoming? Your practice of the Word of God determines the answer.

Redeemed For What Reason?

Ephesians 1:9–12

Introduction:

Christianity must be very confusing to those who don't know it well. Listening to TV is enough to boggle the mind as all sorts of contradictory teaching is given. It would be interesting to see why one would think it good to be saved. But that thought raises an interesting question: what is the purpose of redemption? Why did Christ die for us? Why are we saved? If we can answer that question, we can answer a lot of other questions.

I. The Perversions of Redemption:

A. Escape from hell.
B. Make life better.
C. Praying a prayer.
D. Find a personal peace.
E. Health, wealth, and prosperity.
F. Healing in the atonement.
G. Finding the God we want rather than the God who is there.
H. Doing God a favor.

II. The Provision of Redemption

A. Redemption was determined in eternity past:
   1. By the counsels of triune God.
   2. God even determined who would be saved.
B. Redemption was accomplished on Calvary's cross.
   1. When Christ died, He died for all our sins.
   2. When He died, all our sins were in the future.
   3. When a sinner trusts Christ, all sins are forgiven: past, present, future.
   4. He died to save us not to make salvation available.
C. Redemption is finished, complete, and eternal.

III. The Purpose of Redemption

A. Christ sought glory (John 17:1, 5).
   1. He sought the return of what was rightfully His and had been laid aside.
   2. His glorification required and resulted from the completed work of redemption.
B. The purpose of redemption is the glorification of God (John 17:4; Ephesians 1:12).

C. We are saved to glorify Him:
   1. In our salvation itself (Ephesians 1:6; James 1:18).
   2. In our lives once saved (Ephesians 2:8–10).
   3. In our eternal praise (Ephesians 2:7).

D. The ultimate purpose of salvation: to glorify God.

IV. The Practicalities of Redemption

A. There are many by-products of redemption:
   1. Transformed lives.
   2. Restoration of homes and families.

B. If the purpose of redemption is to glorify God, then it:
   1. Explains circumstances (a matter of how God chooses to allow each of us to glorify Him).
   2. Explains suffering.

C. We lose sight of God's purpose and begin to believe that the purpose of redemption is somehow tied in to our pleasure, etc.

D. This should have a profound effect on our life-style. We are saved to glorify Him not to better our lot in life (man's chief end—to glorify God and enjoy HIM forever).

Conclusion:

Salvation is an incredible blessing to us, but blessing us is not the primary purpose of God. God's glory is most prominent. We must reject anything that does not contribute to the glory of God: all man-centered purposes for redemption, all living outside the confines of His will, and all preoccupation with self.

The Role of Repentance

Luke 17:3

Introduction:

God desires that there be unity and harmony among His people, but He doesn't encourage achieving unity by glossing over differences.

I. Repentance

A. Its relationship to sorrow:
   1. Sorrow may accompany it but it is not the same.
      a. Sorrowful feelings equal regret.
      b. Repentance is not first a feeling.
   2. Sorrow without repentance is common.
   3. Repentance will produce sorrow, but sorrow may come later.

B. Meaning (Luke 22; 32; Isa. 55:7–8):
   1. To turn, to do an about face in thinking that leads to change of life.
   2. Mental alteration of thought that leads to change of life.
   3. Turning from one's own sinful ways and thoughts to a position of Bible holiness.

C. Changes of thinking:
   1. From "I can get away with it" to "God knows all about it."
   2. From "It is good for me or can bring me happiness" to "It will surely ruin me and my happiness" (no genuine child of God can think for long that sin is a pathway to happiness).
   3. From "I can keep this up as long as I want" to "I must stop at once."
   4. From hardened toward God and others to a rekindling of concern.

D. Summary:
   1. Repentance is seeing one's sin as sin.
   2. Repentance is turning from pride to humility (seeing self as unworthy).
   3. Repentance is a prerequisite to forgiveness.
   4. Repentance is the opposite of excuse-making and blame-shifting.
   5. Repentance is the frank admission of wrong thinking that led to wrong doing.

II. Confession

A. Definition:

1. *Con-fessare*—to say along with.
2. Outward expression of inward admission that I am (or was) wrong.
3. A verbal admission of wrong made in the presence of the wronged party.

B. Contractual aspect:

1. Wrongdoer willing to sign contract admitting wrong and committing to non-repetition.
2. No actual contract but very serious aspect of truth.

C. Conditions:

1. No support for Catholic confessional.
2. No support for public confession of private sins.
3. No confession of sin that one isn't sure is sin.
4. No confession of what one isn't guilty of doing.

D. Summary:

1. Confession is admitting what one has been charged with.
2. Confession is first step to reconciliation.

Conclusion:

Repentance stresses that God wants things actually dealt with rather than glossed over. Repentance and confession are necessary for any real forgiveness.

Look unto Me

Isaiah 45:16–25

Introduction:

These verses contain a clear exposition of the doctrine of salvation. They were instrumental in the conversion of Charles Haddon Spurgeon, the great English preacher.

I. The Source of Our Salvation

A. We want to look everywhere but to Him:
   1. To other people.
   2. To institutions.
   3. To ourselves.

B. God says: "Look unto ME" and supports it with:
   1. An expression of who He is.
      a. He is the creator of heavens and earth (v. 18).
      b. He is the only true God there is (v. 18*b*).
      c. He is the only source of revelation (v. 19).
      d. He is the only One able to make correct predictions (v. 21).
      e. He is the sovereign ruler over all things (v. 23).
   2. An expression of the folly of any other approach.
      a. False gods cannot save (v. 20).
      b. False beliefs will yield to Him (v. 23*b*).
      c. False prophets will be ashamed (v. 24*b*).

C. He says, "Look unto Me" and away from anything else.

II. The Substance of Our Salvation

A. "Look"—something incredibly simple and straightforward.

B. The world likes a religion it cannot comprehend.
   1. It does all it can to build that kind of religion.
   2. It is illustrated by Naaman and brazen serpent.

C. This simplicity is designed.
   1. It removes human pride.
   2. It reminds us that everyone is saved the same way.

D. Note carefully:
   1. Doesn't say "see me" but only "look unto me."
   2. "It is looking, not seeing, that saves the sinner."

III. The Scope of Our Salvation

A. Note whom He has called upon to look:
   1. It expands scope incredibly.
   2. It is said in context of Old Testament Judaism.

B. It has various applications:
   1. Geographical.
   2. Figurative (even those furthest away).
C. Whatever will not let you look will be removed the moment you do look.

Conclusion:

Everyone wants to make salvation difficult; God makes it simple. All you need to do is look. Have you? If so, are you sharing that message?

What in the World?

John 3:16

Introduction:

We all talk in clichés to some degree, especially athletes. One cliché has multiple uses. When baffled by what is going on, we say, "What in the world?" When baffled as to reasons, we say "Why in the world?" When boggled by a task, we say, "How in the world?" Those cliches provide a outline for treating John 3:16.

I. **What in the World?**—"that He gave His only begotten Son."
   A. God is the giver.
      1. It is none other than Almighty God Himself.
      2. The Creator/Sustainer becomes the Redeemer.
   B. Jesus is the gift.
      1. Jesus is His Son.
      2. When God gave the Son, He gave Himself.
      3. "Only begotten"—emphasis is on *only*, not begotten.
   C. The giving—Jesus was always the gift of God.
      1. Gave Him when He laid salvation's plan.
      2. Gave Him when He came to earth.
      3. Gave Him when He endured "such contradiction of sinners against Himself."
      4. Gave Him in the sufferings of the final week.
      5. Gave Him on the cross.

II. **Why in the World?**—"For God so loved the world."
   A. Love is the nature of God.
      1. God's love springs from His very nature—"God is love."
      2. He loves because it is His nature to do so.
      3. We need to stress this side of the Father.
   B. Love meets the situation of the world.
      1. It meets its incredible need.
      2. It meets its enormous scope.
      3. It meets our complete inability—there is nothing man could possibly do to satisfy God due to the very nature of God.
   C. "He seemed to love us better than His only Son and did not spare Him that He might spare us."

III. How in the World?—"that whosoever believeth in Him should not perish but have everlasting life."

A. The key issues is belief: faith, trust, or reliance.
   1. One must assent to the truth.
   2. One must accept for one's self.

B. The scope is "whosoever."
   1. It opens door for everyone.
   2. It eliminates any limiting factor.

C. The result is:
   1. Deliverance—should not perish.
   2. Donation—everlasting life.

Conclusion:

God gave His Son to die on the cross because of His great love and the world's great need. This all fits together simply by belief. There are messages here: Do you have the gift of eternal life that God wants you to have? Are you sure of that possession as God wants you to be?

Satan's Seduction

Judges 16:4–22

Introduction:

Samson's story is strange, and it contains only one positive principle: God uses us *in spite of* our sinfulness. It brings us a caution: never say that God uses us *because of* our sinfulness. Notice three lessons along these lines:

I. The Inadequacy of Ability

A. He was a man of great ability.

B. He had serious character flaws.

1. His ability was more than adequate.
2. His character flaws were fatal.

C. These are problems of our day as well.

II. The Degradation of Lust

A. It is an incredible story—hard to understand.

B. Part of story is untold—note the pattern of Samson's life:

1. Woman of Timnath.
2. Harlot at Gaza.
3. Delilah.

C. Lust always:

1. Breaks down resistance.
2. Sears the conscience.
3. Overwhelms the mind.
4. Destroys the judgment.

III. The Insanity of Self-dependence

A. He may have come to believe he was strong apart from his hair.

B. This likely explains much currently going on.

Conclusion:

Have you forgotten the real source of your strength?

The Father of All Lies

John 8:44

Introduction:

Satan is the father of all lies, although he is not necessarily the father of all liars (because some of God's children are liars also). Let's see what the Scripture says:

I. Lying traces its source from Satan.

A. Satan is the author of all lies.

B. Satan doesn't speak the truth unless it is to achieve a false purpose (ex: quoting Scripture at the temptation of Christ).

C. Satan's lies at the outset in Garden of Eden (Gen. 3, note three lies and their nature):

1. His lie by innuendo—"yea, hath God said?"
2. His lie by direct denial—"ye shall not surely die."
3. His lie by questioned motives—"For God doth know . . ."

II. Lying is characteristic of the old nature.

A. The natural tendency of man is to lie (we *are not* naturally truthful—cf. Ps. 58:3).

B. Telling the truth takes a certain amount of effort.

C. This is true of the children of God to the degree we allow the old nature to dominate our lives.

1. New nature promises deliverance from lying.
2. When we get away from the Lord, we allow ourselves to become as bad as the unconverted.
3. When we lie, we voluntarily surrender ourselves to the realm of Satan.

III. Lying is destructive of Christian testimony.

A. The unsaved expect more from God's people and are turned off when they encounter Christians who lie.

1. You may be damaging the testimony of others as well as destroying your own.
2. There is no quicker way to lose credibility with the unconverted than by lying.

B. Lying destroys credibility before the saved.

1. There are those who can never be trusted because of their previous lying.
2. The damage is always done to the one who lies, not to the one who is lied to.

IV. Lying is evidence of spiritual problems.

A. It is obviously a sin—no need for proof here.

B. It can show a variety of problems.

1. Lying is rebellion (believe some liars are not rebels, but have never known a rebel that was not a liar).
2. Lying shows pride—we lie:
   a. To protect ourselves.
   b. To promote ourselves.
   c. To produce desired results.
3. Lying shows a lack of character.
   a. It usually has been tolerated in early years.
   b. Lying generally a sign of weakness.

V. Lying is cured by telling the truth.

A. See Ephesians 4:25.

B. Truth is fairly easy to discern.

1. Truth agrees with the facts.
2. Truth agrees with the Word of God (Rom. 3:4; Titus 1:2).

Conclusion:

Lies are always a matter of choice. They may be habitual, but they are always choice. The cure for lying is to recognize lies for what they are, make right as many as possible, and start telling the truth! Satan is the father of all lies. Have you allowed yourself to become like one of his children?

Prince of Darkness / Angel of Light

2 Corinthians 11:13–15

Introduction:

It is amazing how few people are willing to call things what they are. Paul didn't suffer from such reticence regarding false teaching. He says it is what we should expect given Satan's methods. Have you ever noticed that the voice which calls you to sin sounds more like an angel's than a devil's? No wonder!

I. Satan is always seeking to deceive you.

A. Notice the context of false teachers:
   1. They try to change themselves into apostles.
   2. No wonder—Satan regularly does the same thing.

B. Satan practices self-transformation.

C. There are numerous Biblical examples of this.
   1. Garden of Eden.
   2. Presence of Satan before Lord in Job.
   3. At the temptation of Christ.

D. It points up again the enormous power of Satan.

II. Satan's deception causes many of your problems.

A. It explains power of temptation.
   1. He can change things around just as he can change himself.
   2. It works in several areas:
      a. Makes wrong seem so right.
      b. Makes folly look like wisdom.
      c. Invents specious pretexts for sin.

B. It explains success of false teaching.
   1. He is able to transfer his transforming powers to others.
   2. Even the very elect can be deceived (Matt. 24:24).

C. It explains philosophy of the world.
   1. It is seen in election campaigns.
   2. It is seen in character of those who hold alien philosophies.

III. Satan's deception calls for special defensive steps.

A. Ever be on guard.
   1. Keep Satan in the back of your mind daily.
   2. Realize he is seeking to ambush you.

B. Do not judge by appearances (Prov. 14:12).
   1. The way a thing looks doesn't tell a thing about it.

2. This explains why many are being deceived today.

C. Seek true wisdom and discernment.
   1. The better you know the Word of God, the better able you will be to resist Satanic transformations.
   2. The final test of everything is the Word of God.
      a. There is no other final authority.
      b. This raises the ire of those who are aberrant.

D. Test/try all things (1 Thess. 5:21).
   1. Submit yourself to the authority of Scripture.
   2. Hold things up to the light of Scripture.

E. Exercise your will power.
   1. This is a command (Jas. 4:7).
   2. We are not to shift to God what He has given to us.

F. Ever abide in Christ.
   1. Satan's superior intellect overmatches yours when you try to face him alone.
   2. Don't take what Satan tries to sell you about your own superior powers (Prov. 16:18).

Conclusion:

Don't underestimate your enemy! He can change colors, costumes, and even character right before your very eyes. In your own power you can't get him—he'll get you! Follow Scripture's special defensive steps!

Conversion

Acts 9:1-8

Introduction:

Conversion is a familiar term. We speak of van conversions. They are really not a bad illustration of the Biblical term.

I. The Essence of Conversion

- A. To Turn
  1. From one way or thing to another (Luke 22:32; James 5:19 & 20)
  2. The interior is turned
- B. Manward side of salvation transaction
- C. Momentary action rather than process

II. The Extent of Conversion

- A. Similar to van conversion
  1. Exterior remains essentially same
  2. Interior is turned
- B. Biblical teaching (1 Thessalonians 1:9; 2 Corinthians 5:17)
- C. When man is converted, something happens
  1. Internal change with external signs
  2. Explains situation of "good" people

III. The Examples Of Conversion

- A. Peter—turned in salvation
  1. From self to Christ
  2. From weakness to strength
- B. Paul
  1. From one morality to another
  2. What changed:
     - a. Anger, pride, hatred
     - b. Saw them as vices; came to detest them as vices

IV. The Essentiality Of Conversion

- A. No conversion without some turning
  1. One direction to another
  2. One dominating principle to another
  3. One determination to another
- B. Acts 26:17 & 18
- B. Implications
  1. Salvation is more than praying a prayer
  2. Conversion involves turning
  3. No turn, no conversion

Conclusion:

Have you been converted? What is causing you problems?

The Sufficiency of Scripture

2 Peter 1:3

Introduction:

Current Christianity is filled with confusion concerning relationships and that which is designed to help us with them, counseling. Much of the confusion is caused by a failure to believe or a refusal to accept the sufficiency of Scripture. We expect the world to reject the Word; we don't expect the church to do so. Many Christians do not believe the Word is sufficient. Believe it is sufficient, here are the reasons.

I. The Statement of the Sufficiency of Scripture

A. What does the word "life" mean?
   1. It is usually interpreted "spiritual life."
   2. I don't believe it means that.
      a. This would involve saying same thing twice.
      b. Peter uses general word for "life."
      c. The overall teaching of Scripture supports a general use here (Bible speaks of actions and attitudes, beliefs and behavior, value systems and viewpoints. What is life but all of them put together. The Bible claims to be "book of life").

B. What is the reference source for life?
   1. The Bible—we don't know anything of eternal value apart from it.
   2. It involves two things:
      a. We understand Scripture as we know Him.
      b. We must study Scriptures to understand them.

II. Support for the Sufficiency of Scripture

A. It comes from the nature of our need.
   1. All needs/problems have to do with relationships.
      a. Many are obvious—relationship between people.
      b. Some are not obvious such as things/circumstances.
   2. The Bible is filled with information on how to relate.

B. It comes from the disarray of other sources.
   1. All extant systems of counseling/problem solving are flawed.
   2. This results in all eclectic systems being flawed.

C. It comes from an appeal to logic.

1. The God who created us must surely know how we work.
2. The obvious results of disobedience testify to its sufficiency.
3. The evidence of those who have behaved biblically speaks of its sufficiency.

III. The Scope of the Sufficiency of Scripture

A. It extends to all of life's relationships:
   1. Parent/child
   2. Husband/wife
   3. Sibling/sibling
   4. Employer/employee
   5. Pastor/people
   6. Saint/saint
   7. Saint/sinner

B. It contains everything we need.
   1. It has direct precepts (commandments).
   2. It has derived principles.

C. It confines all our contacts.
   1. We should concentrate on understanding and expounding the meaning of the Word.
   2. We should begin with what the Bible says.
      a. Most Christian systems begin with what some person says.
      b. The Bible is our source—it is not a book of proof-texts.
   3. We should beware of teaching which does not begin with the Bible.

Conclusion:

Make no mistake! The Bible is sufficient for all of life. It is the ultimate "owner's manual." When we turn to other sources, we are sacrificing truth. Let's stand on the sufficiency of Scripture.

The Time of the Rapture

Acts 1:7

Introduction:

Many Bible teachers set dates and times for the coming of the Lord. Every date set thus far has already been proved wrong. What does the Bible say?

I. The Second Coming

A. There are obviously two different events in 1 Thessalonians 4:13–18 and Revelation 19:11–16.

B. Both are called "second coming" (although only the second actually is).

C. The rapture is at issue, but the whole program is in question.

II. What Does the Bible Say?

A. We need to examine various passages.

1. Matthew 24:36–39, 42, 44
2. Matthew 25:13
3. Mark 13:32
4. Luke 12:39–40
5. Acts 1:7
6. 1 Thessalonians 5:1–7
7. Revelation 3:3

B. The biblical teaching is clear.

1. We do not know (are not to know) time of second coming.
2. There are absolutely no signs of the rapture.
3. There is no prophecy being fulfilled right now.
4. There is no prophecy to be fulfilled.
5. There are no things to be made ready.

III. The Point of the Matter

A. If we cannot know, what's the point?

1. Ignorance engenders more expectation.
2. Prophecy is for information; the rapture is to have effects on us.

B. Why second coming teaching?

1. It provides comfort (1 Thess. 4:13, 18).
2. It grants encouragement (Titus 2:13).
3. It encourages justice/equity (James 5:7–9).
4. It stresses faithfulness (1 Thess. 5:7–9).
5. It stimulates service (1 Cor. 15:58).

6. It promotes soul-winning (Acts 1:7–8).
7. It engenders purity (1 John 3:3).

C. If your interest in the future doesn't drive you to the above, then it is nothing more than curiosity and hobbyhorse interest.

Conclusion:

Jesus is coming, but there is no assurance it will be at a particular time. He may come today. Are you ready?

The Promise of His Coming

2 Thessalonians 4:13–5:11

Introduction:

There is much interest in prophetic themes. We are promised that Jesus is coming again, and that promise is a wonderful one.

I. A Comforting Promise (4:18)

A. It assures us of reunion with loved ones.

B. It relieves fears of destruction by nuclear holocaust.

C. It reaffirms that God is sovereignly in control of universe.

D. It declares that Christ's kingdom will yet triumph.

E. It affirms that Satan will ultimately be defeated.

F. It announces that some will not have to experience death.

II. A Cautioning Promise (5:1–3)

I don't believe we are to "play games with prophecy" because:

A. The Bible makes it very clear we can't and aren't to know when Christ is coming.

1. It is the passage's plain teaching.
2. It is illustrated as a thief in the night.

B. There are no signs of His coming of any kind.

1. The next event in the prophetic timetable is the rapture.
2. The rapture may occur at any moment.
3. We are not to know when it will take place.
4. Thus there can't be any signs of it.

C. No one knows exactly how the historic details fit the overall picture.

1. There may be time after rapture before tribulation.
2. Things can happen very fast and without much warning.

D. All attempts to identify signs to this point have proved wrong—which doesn't stop the speculation.

E. Such teaching/preaching tends to make Word of God an object of curiosity which it is not.

F. Such teaching causes us to waste time which might better be spent on other things (Acts 1:8—"why stand ye gazing up?").

III. A Challenging Promise (5:4–8)

The hope of second coming (if it is more than speculation) should produce a response in the believer.

A. It produces personal holiness (1 John 3:3).
   1. We will be concerned for the state in which we will meet Him.
   2. We will deal with issues of Biblical holiness, not just outward appearances. Holiness is a matter of the heart.
   3. Any concern with prophecy that doesn't result in an increase in Biblical holiness is merely curiosity.

B. It produces concern for the lost (Acts 1:8–11).
   1. There is power instead of knowledge in this place.
   2. There are witnesses instead of investigators here.
   3. Any concern with prophecy that doesn't cause us to seek the salvation of the lost is merely curiosity.

Conclusion:

Jesus is coming again! That knowledge should affect our lives significantly. It should cause us to perfect holiness. It should give us a burden for souls—getting people to Jesus. If you are not working on personal holiness and bringing people to Jesus, your belief in the second coming is questionable.

The Scope of Sin

Psalm 66:18

Introduction:

Returned missionaries often have interesting insights. One was asked the greatest problem in the American church, and his answer was somewhat surprising: the backlog of unconfessed sin. Psalm 66:18 says, "If I regard (hold in esteem, see and do nothing about) iniquity. . . the Lord will not hear me!" Surely unconfessed sin involves hindrance to prayer. There are at least six kinds of sin that could be a problem.

I. **Secret Sin (Psalm 19:12)**
   A. It is that which is concealed, hidden.
      1. The idea is "hidden from view, not known to others."
      2. David knew a great deal about this one!
   B. This type of sin has a frightening aspect (Num. 32:23).
      1. "Be sure your sin will track you down."
      2. Unconfessed secret sin is very serious.

II. **Presumptuous Sin (Psalm 19:13)**
   A. It is that which is arrogant, proud, insolent.
      1. It is open, defiant sin.
      2. It is sin for which we intend to ask forgiveness.
   B. Satan has a way of getting us into such situations.

III. **Sins of Commission (1 John 3:4)**
   A. The most common definition of sin is "doing wrong."
      1. Its actual definition: "Any transgression of or want of conformity to the law of God."
      2. It is doing anything that is forbidden.
   B. Because it is the most common, it is also dangerous.
      1. It can lead us to believe we are clear.
      2. We need to recognize it as only part of the picture.

IV. **Sins of Omission (James 4:17)**
   A. It picks up second part of definition.
      1. It is any area in which we fail to do right.
      2. "Ignorance is no excuse if we should know."
   B. It is probably the most searching of all.
      1. It rules out "sinless perfectionism."
      2. It catches every one of us every day.

V. Sins of the Spirit (Luke 15:25-30)

A. It can be seen by example.
   1. The older brother had attitude problem.
   2. The older brother sinned in spirit.

B. It is a very damaging area.
   1. It displeases the Lord and grieves the Holy Spirit.
   2. It may be the most common undealt with sin among Christians (it hinders more prayer and spiritual progress than any other).

VI. Sins of Unbelief

A. A lack of faith is sin for God's people (Rom. 14:23).
   1. It questions character of God.
   2. This is what makes worry sinful.

B. Lack of faith is the ultimate sin for unconverted (Heb. 11:6).
   1. People go to heaven or hell without regard to goodness or badness.
   2. Our eternal destiny based totally on belief.

Conclusion:

You may be experiencing blocked prayer and stunted growth because of unconfessed sin that is "regarded" in you life. That is foolish because forgiveness is so readily available. Will you confess your sin? If you have never trusted Christ, the greatest need you have is to face your sin of unbelief.

The Ultimate Example

2 Corinthians 8:7–9

Introduction:

A TV evangelist believes that Jesus was rich when He was on earth. He holds further that the fact that He was rich proves that He wants us to be rich. This sounds exciting, but is this what the Bible says? What does Jesus want for us relative to finance?

I. The Status of Christian Generosity (v. 7)

A. Let's compare some very important concepts:
   1. Faith—fairly general term here—belief in God.
   2. Utterance—ability to instruct others.
   3. Knowledge—Holy Spirit given knowledge of God and truth.
   4. Diligence—readiness to discharge every duty.
   5. Love—meet needs on deepest level possible.

B. The meaning of the comparison is significant.
   1. The subject—Christian generosity—ranks right up there.
   2. Christian generosity is a part of full-orbed Christianity.
   3. When it is missing, character is incomplete.

II. The Motivation of Christian Generosity (v. 8)

A. "I speak not by commandment."
   1. Paul did not command to give; he used other motives.
   2. "I'm not going to force you to do what I can't persuade you to do."
   3. He appeals to heart, conscience, and judgment.

B. "By occasion of the forwardness of others."
   1. This is another reference to Macedonia.
   2. He reminds them of the example already stated.

C. "To prove the sincerity of your love."
   1. Love to whom? God, Christ, Paul, church, other individuals?
   2. Christian generosity is a mark of love to all five.
   3. If love is meeting needs at the deepest level, then generosity is necessarily involved.

III. The Ultimate Example of Christian Generosity (v. 9)

A. "For ye know the grace of our Lord Jesus Christ."
   1. "He was rich"—speaks of His pre-incarnate state.

2. "He became poor"—speaks of His incarnation.
3. "That ye through His poverty might be made rich"—speaks of salvation.

B. Does Jesus want us rich?
   1. Matthew 6:24—Riches tend to become a master and to pull us away from Christ.
   2. Matthew 6:19–21—The simple commandment is, do not lay up treasures.
   3. Matthew 13:22—Riches tend to be "deceitful"—tell us things which are not accurate or correct.
   4. Matthew 19:21–23—The story of rich young ruler shows:
      a. Riches tend to intrude before Christ.
      b. Riches tend to make it hard to settle kingdom issues.
   5. Mark 8:36–37—Riches can't be compared to spiritual things.
   6. Mark 12:41–44—Christ commends her for giving all she had (tendency today would be to mock her for that).
   7. Luke 6:24—Woe to the rich!
   8. Luke 12:15—Beware of greed!
   9. Luke 6:29–30—Praise Christian generosity!

Conclusion:

The difference between the plans of Jesus and those of many of His followers is remarkable. He had no plan for becoming rich and always spoke with deep earnestness about the dangers attending such attempts. Jesus may or may not want you to be rich, but He surely wants you to be generous.

Worship the Lord

2 Chronicles 16:8–35

Introduction:

This passage focuses on the aspect of worship. Many complain about an absence of worship, but unfortunately we often are not clear on what worship really is. This passage is very instructive on the subject.

I. **The Nature of Worship** (vv. 28–30)
   A. Inadequate definitions:
      1. Subjective feelings or experiences.
      2. Outward performances.
      3. Reverence.
   B. Dictionary definition: declaring God's worth or expressing His praise.
   C. Biblical definition:
      1. Comes from word that is translated both "worship" and "bow down" or "make obeisance."
      2. Outward bowing down that reflects inward bowing.
      3. Inward bowing as a result of recognizing greatness of God, smallness of man, and difference between.
   D. Summary: Worship is an attitude that recognizes the greatness of God and inwardly bows down as a result.

II. **The Manner of Worship** (vv. 8–12)
   There are many ways of doing this that include:
   A. Express gratitude to Him (v. 8*a*).
   B. Pray to Him (v. 8*b*).
   C. Testify to what He has done for you (v. 8*c*).
   D. Sing to Him and about Him (v. 9*a*).
   E. Talk of His wondrous works (v. 9*b*).
   F. Exalt Him (glory in His name) (v. 10*a*).
   G. Rejoice in Him (v. 10*b*).
   H. Call on Him in every time of need (v. 11).
   I. Constantly remind yourself of what He has done, especially in your personal life (v. 12).

III. **The Object of Worship** (vv. 14–22)
   A. He is God (v. 14*a*).
      1. He is a living God.
      2. He is a powerful God (created the heavens and earth).
      3. He is a personal God.
      4. He is an active God.

B. His judgements are being worked out in the earth (v. 14*b*).
C. He keeps His commitments (vv. 15–20).
D. He protects His people (vv. 21–22).

IV. The Impact of Worship (vv. 23–27)
A. Since worship is an internal attitude, we expect it to show in certain attitudes and actions based on it.
B. These would include:
1. Praising the Lord.
2. Rejoicing in the Lord.
3. Submission to the Lord.
4. Obedience to the Lord's Word.
5. Reverence of the Lord's person.
6. Witnessing for Him—best way to share His greatness with others.
7. Praying to Him.
C. They show an important side of worship.
1. Should occur as part of service.
2. Can't be limited to a service.
3. Actually becomes a total way of life.

Conclusion:

Worship surely missing in modern Christianity. Biblical worship actually permeates all of life. Biblical worship is an attitude that would change the way we think and also the way we live. How much do you worship?

In Awe of the Almighty

Psalm 46

Introduction:

This passage is known as "Luther's Psalm." Not only was it the basis for "A Mighty Fortress," but is was his source of encouragement when times were trying and difficult. It is especially helpful in the face of fear. What is it you fear? Everyone has some things!

I. **The Structure of the Psalm** (Note the word *selah* in three places: its basic meaning is "pause" or a rest as in music—came to mean "stop and think of that.")
   A. The premise stated (vv. 1–3).
      1. The focus is on God.
      2. Three things are said of Him: refuge, strength, help.
      3. Particular emphasis is on time of trouble.
   B. The premise supported (vv. 4–7).
      1. The emphasis is on God.
      2. God is with us.
      3. The refuge idea is restated
   C. The premise summarized (vv. 8–11).
      1. Verse 11 repeats verse 7 as a summary of Psalm.
      2. It stresses role of God in the world.
      3. "Lord of hosts"—God of universe; "God of Jacob"—God of the individual, lonely wanderer.

II. **The Scenes of the Psalm**
   A. A castle on a hill.
   B. A collection of natural cataclysms (earthquake, hurricane, typhoon, tornado, tidal wave all at once).
   C. "Jerusalem the golden" (most beautiful, protected city on earth—not subject to earthquakes).
   D. The "Iron Curtain" (split from top to bottom—Europe suddenly healed without human intervention).
   E. An effective bodyguard (Secret Service with Presidents).

III. **The Stresses of the Psalm**
   A. The sovereignty of God.
      1. The power of His word (v. 6*b*)—Same word spoken in creation and by Christ in His earthly ministry.
      2. His power—(vv. 8*b*–9)—both war and peace are His to control and dispense.
      3. His exaltation (v. 10*b*)—"I *will be* exalted."

B. The provision of God.
   1. Refuge (v. 1)—place to which we can escape.
   2. Strength (vv. 1–5)—idea of broken tooth on post.
   3. Help (vv. 1–5)—"Very present"—exceedingly proven.
   4. Presence (v. 7)—closer than our troubles.
   5. Intervention (vv. 5, 6, 8, 9).
   6. Timing (v. 5)—"and that right early"—at the turning of the day—just when needed.

C. The expectations of God.
   1. The control of fear (v. 2).
      a. "Therefore" because of this.
      b. "We will not fear"—statement of fact.
      c. No matter what may happen (uses most extreme scenario possible).
   2. Observing His greatness (v. 8).
      a. See what God has done.
      b. See God in what has been done.
      c. Never forget what God has done in the past.
   3. Silence before Him (v. 10).
      a. "Be still"—let down, relax.
      b. Forego arguing with God.
      c. Wait for Him to speak and act.

Conclusion:

Psalm 46 was written for a nation but tailored to individuals. It has a powerful message for us today. God is to us what He was to Israel and more so. This fact should attack fear, should cause us to be silent before Him, and should cause us to let God be God.